THE POCKET BOOK OF GOLF Jokes

books by
BOXER

www.booksbyboxer.com

Published in the UK by
Books By Boxer, Leeds, LS13 4BS

ISBN: 9781909732537

Golf balls are like eggs... They're white. Sold by the dozen. And a week later you have to buy some more.

A golfer sliced a ball into a field of chickens, striking one of the hens and killing it instantly. He was understandably upset, and sought out the farmer.

“I’m sorry,” he said, “my terrible tee-shot hit one of your hens and killed it.

Can I replace the hen?”

“I don’t know about that,” replied the farmer, mulling it over. “How many eggs a day do you lay?”

Golfer: That can't be my ball, it looks too old.

Caddie: It's been a long time since we started.

After a 2 year study, the National Science Foundation announced the following results on America's ball-related recreational preferences:

- The sport of choice for unemployed people is basketball.
- The sport of choice for maintenance level employees is bowling.
- The sport of choice for blue-collar workers is football.
- The sport of choice for supervisors is baseball.
- The sport of choice for middle management is tennis.
- The sport of choice for corporate officers is golf.

Conclusion: The higher you rise in the corporate structure, the smaller your balls become.

Golfer: This is the worst golf course I've ever played on!

Caddie: This isn't the golf course sir, we left that an hour ago.

Club Pro: I'm sorry sir, we have no tee times available on the course today.

Golfer: What if Arnold Palmer and Jack Nicklaus showed up? I'm sure you'd find a starting time for them.

Club pro: Of course we would, sir.

Golfer: Well, I happen to know they're not coming, so we'll take their time.

Wife: You spend too much time thinking about golf! Do you even remember the day we got married?

Husband: Of course I do! It was the same day I sank that 45ft putt.

Brand new golf balls are attracted to water, and the power of the attraction is in direct proportion to how much the balls cost.

Golfer: Please stop checking your watch all the time, it's distracting!

Caddie: This isn't a watch, sir... it's a compass.

An avid golfer goes to see a fortune teller to enquire if there are any golf courses in heaven.

"Well, I have good news and bad news" she tells the golfer.

"What's the good news?" asks the golfer.

"The good news sir is that the courses in heaven are spectacular, without a doubt better than anything you have EVER seen on earth."

"What's the bad news then?" he asks.

"You have a tee time at 8:30 tomorrow morning."

If you think it's hard to meet new people, pick up the wrong ball on a golf course.

Q: What do golf and sex have in common?

A: They're two things you can enjoy even if you're bad at both of them.

Four old men went into the pro shop after playing 18 holes of golf. The pro asked, "Did you guys have a good game today?"

The first old guy said, "Yes, I had three riders today."

The second old guy said, "I had the most riders ever. I had five."

The third old guy said, "I had 7 riders, the same as last time."

The last old man said, "I beat my old record. I had 12 riders today."

After they went into the locker room, another golfer who had heard the old guys talking about their game went to the pro and said, "I have been playing golf for a long time and thought I knew all the terminology of the game, but what's a rider?"

The pro said, "A rider is when you hit the ball far enough to get in the golf cart and ride to it."

Q: What's a golfer's favourite letter?

A: T!

Player 1: Are you a scratch player?

Player 2: I sure am.
Every time I hit the ball I scratch my head and wonder where it went.

Player 1: How do you like my game?

Player 2: Oh, it's a great game, but personally I prefer golf.

Golf is a game where the ball lies poorly and the golfers lie well.

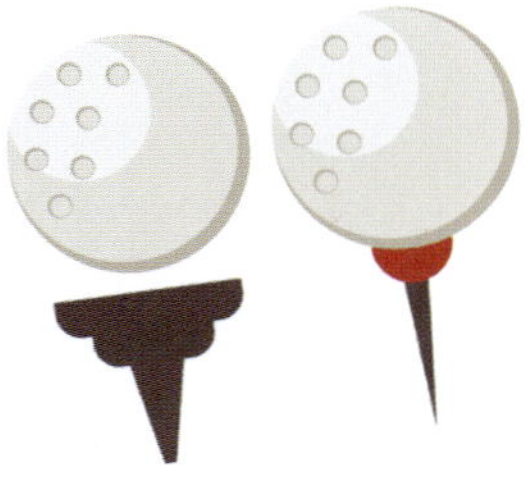

A golfer who says he never cheats is also a liar.

Golfer: I'd move heaven and earth to break 100 on this course.

Caddie: Try heaven. You've already moved most of the earth.

As a couple approaches the altar, the groom tells his wife-to-be, “Honey, I’ve got something to confess: I’m a golf nut, and every chance I get, I’ll be playing golf!”

“Since we’re being honest,” replies the bride, “I have to tell you that I’m a hooker.”

The groom replies, “That’s okay, honey. You just need to learn to keep your head down and your left arm straight.”

The only problem with golf is that the slow groups are always in front of you and the fast groups are always behind you.

After church one Sunday, one of the church goers walked up to his priest and said, "Father, is it a sin to play golf on Sundays?"

"My son," said the priest, putting his hand on the man's shoulder, "I've seen your golf game, it's a sin any day."

The school teacher was taking her first golfing lesson. “Is the word spelt p-u-t or p-u-t-t?” she asked the instructor.

“P-u-t-t is correct,” he replied.

“Put means to place a thing where you want it. Putt means merely a vain attempt to do the same thing.”

What's the difference between a bad golfer and a bad skydiver?

A bad golfer goes:
WHACK..."Damn!"

A bad Skydiver goes:
"Damn!"...WHACK.

What are the four worst words you could hear during a game of golf?

It's still your turn.

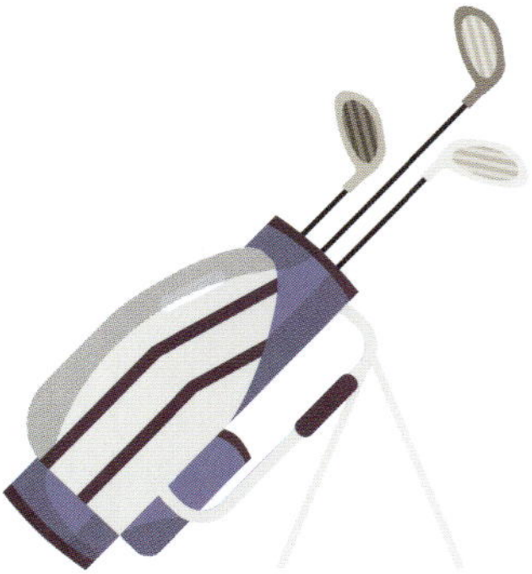

"Your trouble is that you're not addressing the ball correctly."

"Yeah, well I've been polite to the bloody thing for long enough."

The other day I was playing golf and I hit two of my best balls.

I stepped on a rake.

Q: Why did they kick Tarzan out of the golf game?

A: He screamed with every swing.

Q: Why didn't the skeleton play golf?

A: His heart wasn't in it.

Q: Why don't grasshoppers watch golf?

A:They watch cricket instead.

Q: What did one golf ball say to the other golf ball?

A: See you round.

Q: What should you do if your round of golf is interrupted by a lightning storm?

A: Walk around holding your 1-iron above your head, because even Mother Nature can't hit a 1-iron.

Q:Who is the best golf partner to have?

A: One who's always a little bit worse than you.

Q: What does it mean when your golf opponent has trouble remembering whether he shot a six or a seven?

A: It means he probably shot an eight.

Q: Why shouldn't you ever play golf in the jungle?

A: There are too many cheetahs.

Q: What do you call 1000 golfers lined up on a pebble beach holding hands?

A: Pebble Beach Golf Links.

Q: What did the golfer buy from the coffee shop?

A: A cup of tee.

One sunny spring day, there was a foursome of ladies at Cherry Hills Country Club about to play a par three, 165 yards along. Quite suddenly, out from the trees beside the fairway, a streaker bounded across the open expanse of the fairway.

In a gasp, one of the women remarked "Oh my! I think I know that guy. Isn't that Dick Green?"

"No." replied her golfing companion. "I think it's just a reflection from the grass."

Q:What do you call a monkey who wins the masters?

A: A chimpion.

Q:Which golfer can jump higher than the flag?

A: All of them – a flag can't jump.

What's the problem with my golf game?

You're standing too close to the ball... after you hit it.

Q: Why do golf courses get hot after a tournament?

A: Because all the fans have left.

Q: Why did the golfer cross the green?

A: To get to the other side.

A fellow comes home after his regular Saturday golf game and his wife asks why he doesn't include Brian Kennedy in the games anymore.

The husband asks, "Would you want to play with a guy who regularly cheats, swears up a storm over everything, lies about his score, and has nothing good to say about anyone else on the
course - ever?"

"Of course I wouldn't" replies the wife.

"Well," says the husband, "apparently neither does Brian Kennedy."

What do you call a golf ball that goes dead straight down the green after you hit it?

A miracle!

What's the difference between a golf ball and directions?

A man will always look for a golf ball.

What do cricket and golf have in common?

A century is a pretty good score for a bad player in either sport.

Why do golfers have to keep buying golf balls?

Because they don't know how to swim.

Q: Why was Cinderella such a poor golfer?

A: Her coach was a pumpkin.

A land surveyor was tasked with mapping a golf course that was expanding from 9 holes to 18 holes. He needed a stout machete to clear thick brush as he went on. Along the way, he came upon a golf club that an irate player must have hurled into the woods. It was in good condition, so he picked it up and continued on.

When he broke out of the brush onto a putting green, two golfers stared at him in awe. After all, he had a machete in one hand, a golf club in the other, and behind him was a clear-cut swath leading out of the woods.

"There," said one of the golfers, "is a guy who really hates to lose a ball!"

A woman goes into the local newspaper office to see that the obituary for her recently deceased husband is published.
The editor informs her that there is a charge of 50p per word. She pauses, reflects, and then says, "Well then, let it read 'Fred Brown died.'"

Amused at the woman's thrift, the editor tells her that there is a seven-word minimum for all obituaries.

She thinks it over and in a few seconds says, "In that case, let it read, 'Fred Brown died: golf clubs for sale.'"

What does a golfer and a very young child have in common?

They can't count past five.

Q: Why do golfers always lose at cards when playing hearts?

A: All they ever have are clubs.

One golfer asked his friend, "Why are you so late in arriving for your tee time?"

His friend replied, "It's Sunday. I had to toss a coin between going to church or playing golf."

"Yes," continued the friend, "but that still doesn't tell me why you are so late."

"Well," said the fellow, "It took over 25 tosses to get it right!"

Wife: I'm sick and tired of your obsession with golf!

Husband: Why, is it driving a wedge between us?

A priest rushed from church one day to keep a golf date. He was halfway down the first fairway, waiting to hit his second shot, when he heard "Fore!" and a ball slammed into his back. Soon, the golfer who had made the drive was on the scene to offer his apologies. When the priest assured him that he was all right, the man smiled.

"Thank goodness, Father!" he exclaimed.

"I've been playing this game for forty years, and now I can finally tell my friends that I've hit my first holy one!"

A guy came home and was greeted by his wife dressed in very sexy underwear.

"Tie me up," she purred softly, "And you can do anything you want."

So he tied her up and went golfing.

After the honeymoon, the new wife tells her husband, "I think it's time for you to stop playing golf. In fact, you might as well sell all of your clubs."

The husband replies, "You're starting to sound like my ex-wife."

His wife says, "I thought you said you've never been married before?"

The husband says, "I haven't."

Have a good round...
may the fours be with you.

Tommy got a job as a caddy. On his first day he left the house at 5:00am and didn't return until well after dark. His worried mother scolded him fiercely going off with his friends before coming home or calling her first.

"But mum," said the young man "I've been working the whole time."

"I don't make much money carrying golf clubs, but I make a killing backing up the golfers' stories in the clubhouse."

Andy and his wife walked into a dentist's office.
Andy said to the dentist, "Doc, I'm in one heck of a hurry. I have three buddies sitting out in my car waiting for us to go play so forget about the anaesthetic, I don't have time for the gums to get numb. I just want you to pull the tooth, and be done with it!

The dentist thought to himself, "My goodness, this is surely a very brave man asking to have a tooth pulled without using anything to kill the pain."

So the dentist asks him, "Which tooth is it, sir?"

Andy turned to his wife Patricia and said, "Honey, open your mouth and show him!"

A golfer had made an awful shot and tore up a large piece of turf. He picked it up and looking about said, "What shall I do with this?"

"If I were you," said the caddie, "I'd take it home to practice on."

An old member died and in his will was a request for his ashes to be scattered in the par 3 hole on top of the hill, because in years of being a member he had never had a hole in one on that hole.

The committee granted permission, so his family, the committee and several club members gathered at the hole and stood with their heads bowed.

The vicar said a few words, took the lid off the urn and started to pour. At that moment, the wind came up and blew him into the bunker.

Golfer: The doctor says I can't play golf.

Caddy: Oh! So he has also played with you?

One fine day, John and Don are out golfing when John slices his ball deep into a wooded ravine. He grabs his 7-iron and proceeds down the embankment into the ravine in search of his ball.
The brush is quite thick, but he searches diligently and suddenly he spots something shiny. As he gets closer, he realizes that shiny object is in fact a 7-iron in the hands of a skeleton lying near an old golf ball.
John excitedly calls out to his golfing partner, "Hey Don, come here. I've got some real trouble down here."

Don comes running over to the edge of the ravine and calls out: "What's the matter, John? Is everything okay?"

John shouts back in a nervous voice, "Throw me my 8-iron! Apparently you can't get out of here with a seven"

A man got on a bus with both of his front pant pockets full of golf balls, and sat down next to a beautiful blonde. The blonde kept looking quizzically at him and his obviously bulging pants. Finally, after many such glances from her, he said "It's golf balls."

The blond looked at him compassionately and said, "Oh you poor thing. I bet that hurts a whole lot worse than tennis elbow?"

A woman arrived at a party. While scanning the guests, she spotted an attractive man standing alone. She approached him, smiled and said, "Hello. My name is Carmen."

"That's a beautiful name," he replied. "Is it a family name?"

"No," she replied. "As a matter of fact I gave it to myself. It represents the things that I enjoy the most – cars and men. Therefore I chose 'Carmen'"

"What's your name?" she asked.

He answered "B. J. Titsengolf."

Q: Why is the game called 'golf'?

A: Because all the other Fore-letter words were already taken.

A guy on holiday finishes his round, and goes into the clubhouse. The head pro says, "Did you have a good time out there?"

The man replied "Fabulous, thank you."

"You're welcome," said the pro. "How did you find the greens?"

The man replied "Easy. I just walked to the end of the fairways and there they were!"

What is the difference between a golfer and a fisherman?

When a golfer lies, he doesn't have to bring anything home to prove it.

What's the difference between a G-spot and a golf ball?

A man will actually search for a golf ball.

A bride and groom stood at the alter, waiting to be married. The bride looked down and saw a set of golf clubs at the groom's feet. "What on earth are you doing with those golf clubs?" she whispered.

"Well," he said, "This won't take all afternoon will it?"

Two golfers are ready to play on the 11th tee as a funeral cortege passes by. The first player stops, doffs his cap and bows his head as the cortege passes.

"That was a really nice thing to do," the second golfer says. "It's good to see there is still some respect in the world"

"Well it's only right," the first golfer replies. "I was married to her for 35 years"

Why do Golfers always carry two pairs of trousers?

In case they get a hole in one!

How many golfers does it take to change a light bulb?

Fore!

A golf club walks into a local bar and asks the barman for a pint of beer. The barman refuses to serve him.

"Why not," asks the golf club.

"You'll be driving later" replies the bartender.

Two Mexican detectives were investigating the murder of Juan Gonzalez.

'How was he killed?' asked one detective.

"With a golf gun," the other detective replied.

"A golf gun? What's a golf gun?"

"I don't know, but it sure made a hole in Juan."

Husband says to his wife, "See you honey, I am off to play Hit and Cuss."

"Hit and Cuss? What's that?" she asked.

He answered, "Well, some people call it golf."

One day, these two men were playing a round of golf. Two women were playing in front of them very slowly. The first guy turns to his friend and says, "Hey, I'm going to ask those ladies if they mind letting us play ahead."

He begins walking over, stops halfway, and returns, saying, "We've got a problem. One of those women is my wife, the other my mistress."

His buddy replies, "That's okay, I'll go talk to them."

He walks over and promptly returns. "Well," he says, "looks like we've got the same problem."

A lion would never drive while drunk.

But a tiger wood.

Four senior golfers hit the course, some of them with waning enthusiasm for the sport.

"These hills are getting steeper as the years go by," one complained.

"These fairways seem to be getting longer too," said one of the others.

"The sand traps seem to be bigger than I remember them too," said the third senior.

After hearing enough from his senior buddies, the oldest, and the wisest of the four of them at 87 years old, piped up and said, "Quit your complaining and just be thankful we're still
on the RIGHT SIDE of the grass!"

Q: Why was the computer so good at golf?

A: Because it had a hard drive.

Do you know why the golf pro tells you to keep your head down while swinging?

It's so you can't see him laughing.

A Father challenged his boastful son to a game of golf. The father was determined to beat his son in golf for the first time. On the very first swing, the son got a hole in one.

"Okay, nice shot son," said the father, thinking quickly on his feet. "Now I will take my practice shot and then we will start."

Two women were put together as partners in the club tournament and met on the putting green for the first time.

After introductions, the first golfer asked, "What's your handicap?"

"Oh, I'm a scratch golfer," the other replied.

"Really!" exclaimed the first woman, suitably impressed that she was paired up with her.

"Yes, I write down all my good scores and scratch out the bad ones!"

A golfer called one of the caddies and asked, "I need a caddy who can count and keep the score. What's 3 and 4 and 5 come to?"

"10" said the caddy.

"Great, you'll do perfectly!"

Fred and George step up to the first tee, one said to the other, "Hey guess what, I got a set of golf clubs for my wife."

To which the other replies "What a great swap!"

In primitive society, when native tribes beat the ground with clubs and yelled, it was called witchcraft; Today, in civilised society, it is called golf.

A lady golfer ran into the clubhouse screaming, "HELP, HELP! I've been stung by a bee and I'm allergic!"

The golf pro responded, "Where?"

The lady answered "Between the first and second hole!"

The pro stated, "your stance is too wide."

What are the 3 rules of Golf? If the ball goes right it's a slice, if the ball goes left it's a hook, and if the ball goes straight it's a miracle!

Golf rules for beginners:

1) Back straight, knees bent, feet shoulder width apart.
2) Form a loose grip.
3) Keep your head down.
4) Avoid a quick back swing.
5) Stay out of the water.
6) Try not to hit anyone.
7) If you are taking too long, please let others go ahead of you.
8) Don't stand directly in front of others.
9) Quiet please ... while others are preparing to go.
10) Don't take extra strokes.

Now, that's very good. Flush the urinal, go outside, and tee off.

A puzzled golfer watched a fellow member don some very unorthodox gear in the clubroom. “How long have you been wearing a corset?” he asked.

“ever since my wife found it in the car.” was the reply.

Golfer: Do you think my game is improving?

Caddie: Absolutely! You miss the ball much closer than you used to.